Collins

Livemocha **ACTIVE FRENCH**

HarperCollins Publishers
77–85 Fulham Palace Road
London W6 8JB
Great Britain

www.collinslanguage.com

First edition 2011

Reprint 10 9 8 7 6 5 4 3 2 1 0
© HarperCollins Publishers 2011

ISBN (UK edition) 978-0-00-737351-2
ISBN (export edition) 978-0-00-741977-7
ISBN (US edition) 978-0-87779-555-1

Collins® is a registered trademark of HarperCollins Publishers Limited

A catalogue record for this book is available from the British Library

Typeset by Macmillan Publishing Services

Audio material recorded and produced by Networks SRL, Milan

Printed and Bound in China by Leo Paper Products Ltd.
Series Editor: Rob Scriven

INTRODUCTION

Welcome to your Livemocha Active French experience! This new course goes above and beyond what a traditional book-based course can offer. With its focus on online learning, Active French provides the opportunity not just to study but to experience the language for yourself by interacting with native speakers online.

Why go online?

Studying a language online allows you to learn in a more natural atmosphere – watching people interact in a **video** is far more lifelike than listening to conversations on a CD. After watching a video dialog, you will be walked through an explanation of some of the **grammar** and **vocabulary** items that were introduced in the new dialog. Then, by completing a variety of **interactive quizzes**, the system will instantly be able to tell you how well you are doing. You can then **talk online** with native French speakers to practice what you've learned.

Who else is online?

Livemocha boasts over 7 million members and is growing every day. These members are online for the same reason as you – to learn and experience a new language. Native French-speaking members will be happy to read through your written and spoken submissions and to give you feedback on how you're doing. You can also connect with people who want to chat in any given language – interaction on an informal, nonacademic basis is an ideal way for you to perfect your language skills.

What do the books do?

The four accompanying books are designed to complement the online course – the dialogs for all of the videos that you can watch online are available here for you to study whenever you don't have access to the Internet. You will also find all of the Grammar and Vocabulary sections explained in the books, plus the culture notes to teach you a little about France.

LEVEL 1

This book is the first of four. It corresponds with Level 1 of the online course.

Level 1 is ideal for students who are newcomers to the language or for those who need to start from the basics.

What you will learn
- How to talk about yourself and where you are from
- How to make introductions, understand suggestions and give instructions
- How to use articles, form questions, express preferences and make comparisons
- How to form the present tense
- Vocabulary for numbers, food and drink, public transport, time and days of the week

 Every time you see this coffee cup symbol in these books, it indicates the presence of a pathway – a guide to exactly where you can find that particular piece of content online. Log on at www.livemocha.com and follow the path to find the online version of what you are studying in the book.

Video Dialog

Pascal and Mélinda sit down for a tea and get to know one another a little better.

 Active French: Level 1 > Unit 1 > Lesson 2 > Video dialog

1

Lesson 1: Nice to meet you 1

- » How to introduce yourself:
  Je m'appelle.
- » How to say where you are from:
  Je suis de.
- » How to say what nationality you are
  Je suis américain(e).

Lesson 2: Nice to meet you 2

- » How to say what you would like:
  Je voudrais.
- » How to say what you do:
  Je suis photographe / étudiant(e)
- » How to say where you work / study:
  Je travaille à Paris.

○ **Collins** | Livemoc

UNIT 1 › LESSON 1

Nice to meet you 1

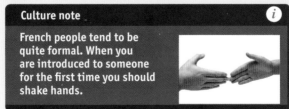

Culture note

French people tend to be quite formal. When you are introduced to someone for the first time you should shake hands.

Video Dialog

Pascal and Mélinda bump into one another and strike up a conversation.

 Watch the video dialog online at
Active French: Level 1 > Unit 1 > Lesson 1 > Video dialog

Pascal:	*Excusez-moi!*
Mélinda:	*Pardon!*
Pascal:	*Bonjour, je m'appelle Pascal. Et vous, comment est-ce que vous vous appelez?*
Mélinda:	*Bonjour. Je m'appelle Mélinda.*
Pascal:	*Vous êtes française?*
Mélinda:	*Non, je suis suisse. Je suis de Lausanne, et vous?*
Pascal:	*Je suis français. Je suis de Lyon. Vous voulez un café?*
Mélinda:	*Je veux bien.*

Pascal:	Excuse me!
Mélinda:	Sorry!
Pascal:	Hello, I'm Pascal. And you, what's your name?
Mélinda:	Hello. I'm Mélinda.
Pascal:	Are you French?
Mélinda:	No, I'm Swiss. I'm from Lausanne, and you?
Pascal:	I'm French. I'm from Lyon. Would you like a coffee?
Mélinda:	Yes, I would.

Grammar

....

In this section we go over some of the grammar points introduced in the dialog.

 Go to Active French: Level 1 > Unit 1 > Lesson 1 > Grammar to listen to these explanations and to access some interactive practice activities.

1 ›   Excuse me!

If you bump into someone you can say:

> *Oh, excusez-moi!*   or   *Pardon!*

You can also use *Excusez-moi* to get someone's attention:

> *Excusez-moi, comment est-ce que vous vous appelez?*
>
> Excuse me, what's your name?

2 › Who are you? Giving your name

To introduce yourself, instead of just saying "I'm Pascal," in French you say "I am called Pascal": *Je m'appelle Pascal*.

> Pascal: *Je m'appelle Pascal.*
> Mélinda: *Je m'appelle Mélinda.*

je m'appelle	I'm called
tu t'appelles	you're called
il / elle s'appelle	he / she's called
nous nous appelons	we're called
vous vous appelez	you're called
ils / elles s'appellent	they're called

3 › Accented letters

Some French letters have accents on them. Some accents change the sound of the letter. For example, the letter *e* with an acute accent (*é*) is pronounced "ay": *un café*.

4 › **You**

In French, there are two ways of addressing someone: you can use the *vous* form when talking to someone you don't know well, or someone who is older than you, or you can use the *tu* form when talking to someone you know well or a child.

Pascal and Mélinda have just met so they are still using *vous* when speaking to each other. In the *vous* form most verbs end in *-ez*.

> *Comment est-ce que vous vous appelez?*
> What's your name?

> *Vous voulez un café?*
> Would you like a coffee?

If they knew each other better, they could use *tu*:

> *Tu veux un café?*
> Would you like a coffee?

5 › ## Who are you? Asking someone's name

If you want to ask someone their name you say:

> *Comment est-ce que vous vous appelez?*
> What's your name?

This is the *vous* form that you use with older people or people you don't know well. If you were asking a child you would use the *tu* form:

> *Comment est-ce que tu t'appelles?*

6 › ## Saying what nationality you are

To say what nationality you are, you say: *Je suis* – I am

> Mélinda: *Je suis suisse.*
> Pascal: *Je suis français.*

A woman would say: *Je suis française.*

In French, words usually take an *-e* ending if they refer to a woman. When words end in *-en*, the *-n* is doubled before the final *-e*. Look at the masculine and feminine forms below.

masculine	feminine
américain	*américaine*
anglais	*anglaise*
australien	*australienne*
canadien	*canadienne*
espagnol	*espagnole*
français	*française*
italien	*italienne*

Note that, in French, nationality adjectives don't start with a capital but with a lowercase letter.

7 › Where are you from?

To say where you are from you say *Je suis de …* – I come from …

> Mélinda: *Je suis de Lausanne, et toi?*
> Pascal: *Je suis français. Je suis de Lyon.*

When the place name starts with a vowel, note that *de* becomes *d'*.

> ### Je suis d'Atlanta.
> I'm from Atlanta.

Most names of towns are the same – although sometimes pronounced slightly differently:

> *Je suis de New York.*
> *Je suis de Washington.*
> *Je suis de Los Angeles.*
> *Je suis de Toronto.*

But some are different:

Londres	London
Moscou	Moscow
Montréal	Montreal

8 ›   I am

être is the verb "to be."

The verb *être* has fairly irregular forms. You don't need to learn them all at one time, but this will help you to recognize them when you hear them.

être

je suis	I am
tu es	you are
il / elle est	he / she is
nous sommes	we are
vous êtes	you are
ils / elles sont	they are

 # Vocabulary

In this section you will learn some useful words and expressions from the dialog.

Go to Active French: Level 1 > Unit 1 > Lesson 1 > Vocabulary to listen to each of the words being pronounced and to access some interactive practice activities.

Oh, excusez-moi!
Excuse me!

Pardon!
Excuse me!

La Suisse
Switzerland

Les États-Unis
The United States

Le Canada
Canada

L'Angleterre
England

La Grande-Bretagne
Great Britain

L'Australie
Australia

La France
France

UNIT 1 › LESSON 2
Nice to meet you 2

Culture note ⓘ

The French drink more coffee than tea. This is due to the fact that historically more of the French overseas territories grew coffee rather than tea, so the French developed more of a taste for coffee.

Nowadays tea is widely drunk, usually with lemon. Many people like herbal teas for their medicinal properties.

A cup of herbal tea is called: *une tisane*.

19

▶ *Video Dialog*

Pascal and Mélinda sit down at a café and get to know one another a little better.

Active French: Level 1 > Unit 1 > Lesson 2 > Video dialog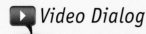

Waiter:	*Bonjour messieurs dames. Qu'est-ce que je vous sers?*
Pascal:	*Bonjour monsieur. Un café et ... Vous voulez un café?*
Mélinda:	*Non, je voudrais un thé, s'il vous plaît.*
Waiter:	*Un thé au citron ou un thé au lait?*
Mélinda:	*Un thé au citron, s'il vous plaît.*
Waiter:	*Un café et un thé au citron.*
Mélinda:	*Vous faites quoi dans la vie?*
Pascal:	*Je suis photographe. Je travaille à Paris, et vous?*
Mélinda:	*Je suis étudiante. Je fais un stage à Paris.*
Waiter:	*Voilà un thé et un café.*

....

Waiter:	Good morning. What can I get you?
Pascal:	Good morning. Coffee and ... Do you want coffee?
Mélinda:	No, I would like tea, please.
Waiter:	Tea with lemon or tea with milk?
Mélinda:	Tea with lemon, please.
Waiter:	Coffee and tea with lemon.
Mélinda:	What do you do for a living?

Pascal:	I'm a photographer. I work in Paris, and you?
Mélinda:	I'm a student. I'm doing work experience in Paris.
Waiter:	There you are, a tea and a coffee.

Grammar

. . . .

 Active French: Level 1 > Unit 1 > Lesson 2 > Grammar

1 › **Saying what you would like**

Pascal asks:

> *Vous voulez un café?*
> Do you want coffee?

And Mélinda answers:

> *Je voudrais un thé.*
> I would like tea.

21

Je voudrais is a polite way of asking for something. Using the present form *je veux* (I want) would be a bit rude. Note that in French there is always a determiner (in this case *un* or *une*) in front of the word for coffee, tea, etc.

2 › | **Tea with milk or tea with lemon**

Mélinda asks for tea with lemon:

> *un thé au citron*
> tea with lemon

When referring to a single serving, there is a determiner (in this case, *un*) in front of the noun. Note the word *au* (or *à la* depending on the word that follows), which is used to introduce an added ingredient.

> *un thé au lait*   tea with milk
> *un thé à la vanille*   vanilla tea
> *un café au lait*   coffee with milk

You'll learn more about *au* and *à la* in further units.

3 › **Saying what you do (1)**

When saying what you do for a living, you use *je suis* (I am) followed by your profession / occupation. Note that in French there is no determiner (in this case no *un* or *une*) in front of the profession.

Pascal: *Je suis photographe.*
I'm a photographer.

Mélinda: *Je suis étudiante.*
I'm a student.

4 › **Saying what you do (2)**

In French, all nouns have a gender and are either masculine or feminine. Feminine nouns often have a different form from the masculine and often end in *-e*.

A male student would say:

Je suis étudiant.
I'm a student.

but Mélinda, being a woman, says:

> *Je suis étudiante.*
> I'm a student.

Other words which behave like *étudiant / étudiante* are:

masculine	feminine	
consultant	*consultante*	consultant
représentant	*représentante*	representative

5 ›   **Saying what you do (3)**

Words for jobs which end in *-en*: change the ending to *-enne* in the feminine. Look at the masculine and feminine forms below.

masculine	feminine	
informaticien	*informaticienne*	computer programmer
mécanicien	*mécanicienne*	mechanic
musicien	*musicienne*	musician
comédien	*comédienne*	actor / actress

6 › **Saying what you do (4)**

Some nouns don't just take an *-e* in the feminine. Some nouns have quite a different ending in the female form. Look at the masculine and feminine forms below.

masculine	feminine	
acteur	*actrice*	actor / actress
coiffeur	*coiffeuse*	hairdresser
directeur	*directrice*	director
serveur	*serveuse*	waiter / waitress
vendeur	*vendeuse*	salesclerk

7 › **Saying what you do (5)**

Some words for jobs are the same for men and women:

le / la comptable	accountant
le / la photographe	photographer
le / la dentiste	dentist

and some words are masculine even though they apply to both men and women:

le médecin	male / female doctor
l'avocat	male / female lawyer

8 › Saying where you work / study

To say where you work, study or live, use *à* in front of the name of the city, town or village.

Je travaille à Paris. I work in Paris.

Je travaille à New York. I work in New York.

Je suis étudiant à Paris. I'm a student in Paris.

Vocabulary Professions

 Active French: Level 1 > Unit 1 > Lesson 2 > Vocabulary

un professeur
teacher (male or female)

Il est professeur de français.
He's a French teacher.

un / une sécretaire
secretary

Sa secrétaire est irlandaise.
His secretary is Irish.

un / une journaliste
journalist

Ce journaliste voyage partout dans le monde.
This journalist travels all over the world.

un agent de police
police officer

L'agent de police a interrogé les témoins.
The police officer interviewed the witnesses.

une infirmière
nurse

Elle est infirmière dans un service d'urgences.
She's an ER nurse.

une institutrice
primary school teacher

Elle est institutrice dans une école primaire de Lyon.
She's a teacher in a primary school in Lyon.

un serveur
waiter

Le serveur apporte les cafés.
The waiter brings the coffee.

une vendeuse
salesclerk

Demande le prix à la vendeuse.
Ask the salesclerk for the price.

un médecin
doctor (male or female)

Je suis malade, appelle le médecin.
I'm not well. Call the doctor.

2

Lesson 1: Greetings at the elevator

» How to greet different people:
Bonjour Delphine!, Bonjour monsieur!

» How to say "Good morning. How are you?": *Bonjour. Comment allez-vous?*

» How to say "Mr." and "Mrs.":
Monsieur, Madame.

Lesson 2: At the café

» How to ask for a coffee:
Je prends un café.

» How to say "a": *un, une.*

» How to say please and thank you:
s'il vous plaît; merci.

◌ **Collins** | Livemocha™

UNIT 2 › LESSON 1

Greetings at the elevator

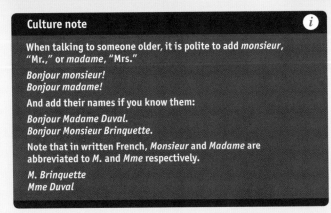

Culture note ⓘ

When talking to someone older, it is polite to add *monsieur*, "Mr.," or *madame*, "Mrs."

Bonjour monsieur!
Bonjour madame!

And add their names if you know them:

Bonjour Madame Duval.
Bonjour Monsieur Brinquette.

Note that in written French, *Monsieur* and *Madame* are abbreviated to *M.* and *Mme* respectively.

M. Brinquette
Mme Duval

Video Dialog

Three neighbors run into one another one morning by the elevator.

Active French: Level 1 > Unit 2 > Lesson 1 > Video dialog

Hugo:	*Bonjour Delphine.*
Delphine:	*Bonjour Hugo.*
Hugo:	*Ça va?*
Delphine:	*Oui, ça va bien, merci, et toi?*
Hugo:	*Oh oui, ça va. L'ascenseur est en panne.*
Delphine:	*Encore! Il est toujours en panne. Bonjour Mme Duval.*
Mme Duval:	*Bonjour Delphine.*
Delphine:	*Comment allez-vous?*
Mme Duval:	*Je vais bien, merci. Bonjour M. Brinquette. Comment allez-vous?*
Hugo:	*Ça va, merci.*
Delphine:	*L'ascenseur est en panne.*
Hugo:	*Tu veux un café? Je t'invite.*
Delphine:	*Oui, je veux bien.*
Hugo:	*Allons au café d'en face.*

Hugo:	Hello Delphine.
Delphine:	Hello Hugo.
Hugo:	How's things?

33

Delphine:	Fine thanks, and you?
Hugo:	Yes, fine. The elevator's broken.
Delphine:	Again! It's always broken. Good morning, Mrs. Duval.
Mrs. Duval:	Good morning, Delphine.
Delphine:	How are you?
Mrs. Duval:	I'm fine, thank you. Good morning, Mr. Brinquette. How are you?
Hugo:	I'm fine, thanks.
Delphine:	The elevator is broken.
Hugo:	Would you like a coffee? It's on me.
Delphine:	Yes, I'd love one.
Hugo:	Let's go to the café across the road.

Culture note ⓘ

When friends meet, it is normal for two female friends, or a man and a woman, to "air kiss." It is called *se faire la bise*. Male friends usually shake hands every time they meet, but some may give each other *la bise* too. The number of times you "air kiss" depends on the area of France you live in. It is normally two, one on each side, but in Paris it may be three or even four kisses. When you meet a family, it can take quite a long time to greet everyone in the appropriate way as children are always greeted properly too!

Grammar

....

 Active French: Level 1 > Unit 2 > Lesson 1 > Grammar

1 › | **Saying hello!**

The usual way of saying "hello" in French is to say *Bonjour* – Good day. There aren't separate expressions for "good morning" or "good afternoon." *Bonjour* is used at any time of day. After about 5 p.m. people usually say *Bonsoir* – Good evening.

2 › Asking how someone is

There is a simple way to ask how someone is doing: you ask *ça va?* – how are you?

> *Bonjour Hugo, ça va?*
> Hi Hugo, how are you?

> *Bonjour Delphine. Ça va?*
> Hello Delphine. How are things?

Ça va? as a question ends on a rising tone.

3 ›

Saying how you are

The answer to *ça va?* is usually the same as the question, but note the difference in the intonation. *Ça va* meaning "I'm fine" ends on a falling tone.

Ça va?
How are you?

Ça va.
I'm fine.

or you can say:

Ça va bien, merci.
I'm well, thanks.

or:

Ça va très bien, merci.
I'm very well, thank you.

4 › Asking how someone is and saying how you are

When Delphine asks Mme Duval how she is, she uses a more polite form:

> *Comment allez-vous?*
> How are you?

and Mme Duval replies:

> *Je vais bien, merci.*
> I am fine, thank you.

If you are talking to an older person or someone you don't know well, always opt for the polite *vous* form. But don't worry too much if you use the *tu* form when you should be using the *vous* form.

5 › ## Using intonation to ask questions

In unit 1, you learned how to ask questions using *est-ce que*. Another simple way of asking questions, as we've seen in this unit with *ça va?*, is to raise the intonation at the end of a sentence. The intonation is the only thing that differentiates the question from the equivalent statement. Look at the sentences below and compare:

Elle veut un café.	She wants a coffee.
Tu veux un café?	Do you want a coffee?
L'ascenseur est en panne.	The elevator is broken.
L'ascenseur est en panne?	Is the elevator broken?

This way of asking questions is mostly used in spoken French.

6 › ## *Vouloir:* "to want"

je veux	I want
tu veux	you want
il / elle veut	he / she wants
nous voulons	we want
vous voulez	you want
ils / elles veulent	they want

Vocabulary

Bonjour
Hello

Bonjour madame.
Hello. (to a lady)

Bonjour monsieur.
Hello. (to a man)

Ça va?
How are you?

Ça va? Oui, ça va bien, merci.
How are you? Fine, thanks.

Comment allez-vous?
How are you?

Comment allez-vous? Je vais bien, merci.
How are you? I'm fine, thanks.

l'ascenseur
elevator

L'ascenseur est en panne.
The elevator is not working.

un café
a coffee

Voulez-vous un café?
Do you want a coffee?

un café
a café

le café d'en face
the café across the street

UNIT 2 › LESSON 2

At the café

Culture note

In France quite a lot of people stop at a bar or café for their breakfast, or more often for a quick coffee on the way to work. A favorite breakfast is a coffee and a croissant or some baguette (a stick of bread sliced down the middle and cut into chunks) with butter and jam.
Breakfast is called *le petit déjeuner* – the little lunch.

When you go to a café and order *un café* or *un express* you get a small espresso cup (you may also hear *un expresso*). If you want another type of coffee, for example with milk in it, you have to ask for *un café crème* or *un grand crème*.

Video Dialog

....

Hugo and Delphine go for a coffee.

Active French: Level 1 > Unit 2 > Lesson 2 > Video dialog

Hugo:	*Bonjour monsieur.*
Waiter:	*Bonjour messieurs dames. Qu'est-ce que je vous sers?*
Hugo:	*Un express pour moi.*
Delphine:	*Et un crème pour moi, s'il vous plaît.*
Hugo:	*Vous avez des croissants?*
Waiter:	*Bien sûr.*
Hugo:	*Tu veux un croissant, Delphine?*
Delphine:	*Non, merci.*
Hugo:	*Un express, un crème et un croissant.*
Waiter:	*C'est tout?*
Hugo:	*Oui, c'est tout.*
Delphine:	*Merci pour le café.*
Hugo:	*Au revoir Delphine. À plus!*
Delphine:	*À plus ... Au revoir monsieur.*
Waiter:	*Au revoir et bonne journée.*

....

Hugo:	Hello.
Waiter:	Hello. What can I get you?
Hugo:	An espresso for me.

Delphine:	And a coffee with milk for me, please.
Hugo:	Do you have any croissants?
Waiter:	Of course.
Hugo:	Do you want a croissant, Delphine?
Delphine:	No, thanks.
Hugo:	One espresso, one coffee with milk and one croissant.
Waiter:	Is that everything?
Hugo:	Yes, that's everything.
Delphine:	Thanks for the coffee.
Hugo:	Bye Delphine. See you!
Delphine:	See you ... Goodbye.
Waiter:	Goodbye and have a good day!

 # *Grammar*

 Active French: Level 1 > Unit 2 > Lesson 2 > Grammar

1 › Ladies and gentlemen!

It is normal for a stranger or someone you don't know very well to say *bonjour monsieur* or *bonjour madame*, but if you are with a group of people you will probably be greeted with *bonjour messieurs dames* or just *messieurs dames*.

> **Bonjour messieurs dames.**
> Good morning, everyone.

2 › **Qu'est-ce que ... ?   What ... ?**

When you hear this you know you are being asked a question. It corresponds to "What" followed by a number of possibilities like: what is..., what can..., what do...? It is an easy way for you to begin a question.

Qu'est-ce que je vous sers?	What can I get you?
Qu'est-ce que vous voulez?	What do you want?
Qu'est-ce que c'est?	What is it?

3 › **a**

In French all nouns are either masculine or feminine. *un* is the word for "a" with masculine nouns. *une* is the word for "a" with feminine nouns. These are all masculine words so "a" is *un*:

un café	a coffee
un express	a small black coffee (espresso)
un crème	a large coffee with milk
un déca	a decaffeinated coffee
un thé	a cup of tea

But if you were asking for a lemonade, you would ask for *une limonade* because *limonade* is feminine.

> ### *Alors un express, un crème et un croissant.*
> An espresso, a coffee with milk and a croissant.

> ### *Et pour moi une limonade.*
> And a lemonade for me.

4 ›   *des croissants*

In French you can't just say "Do you have croissants?" You have to add *des* in front of the plural word and ask:

> ### *Vous avez des croissants?*
> Do you have any croissants?

> ### *Vous avez des timbres?*
> Do you have any stamps?

5 ›   Please and thank you

S'il vous plaît means "please." You use *s'il vous plaît* when you are
talking to someone older or someone you don't know well. You use
s'il te plaît when talking to a friend or someone you know well. *Merci*
means "thank you." *Non, merci* means "no, thank you."

Hugo:	*Un express, un crème et un croissant, s'il vous plaît. Tu veux un croissant, Delphine?*
	An espresso, a coffee with milk and a croissant, please. Do you want a croissant, Delphine?
Delphine:	*Non, merci.*
	No, thank you.

6 › **For me!**

Pour means "for."

pour moi	for me
pour toi	for you
pour vous	for you
Merci pour le café.	Thanks for the coffee.

The waiter could also say:

> *Et pour vous madame, ce sera quoi?*
> And what would you like to drink / eat, madam?

7 › **Is that everything?**

> *C'est tout?*
> Is that everything?

> *C'est tout.*
> That's everything.

You change the words *c'est tout* from a statement into a question by raising your voice at the end.

8 › Goodbye

au revoir means "goodbye." *à plus tard* means "see you later." But among friends people often say *à plus* which is short for *à plus tard*. When parting with someone, you'll also hear:

à demain till tomorrow

Bonne journée! Have a good day!

Bonne après-midi! Have a good afternoon!

And in the evening:

Bonne soirée.

Have a good evening.

Or later:

Bonne nuit!

Good night!

Vocabulary

Active French: Level 1 > Unit 2 > Lesson 2 > Vocabulary

un express
an espresso

Je voudrais un express.
I would like an espresso.

un crème
a coffee with milk

Delphine veut un crème.
Delphine wants a coffee with milk.

un déca
a decaf

Je prends un déca.
I'll have a decaf.

un croissant
a croissant

Hugo veut un croissant.
Hugo wants a croissant.

un chocolat chaud
a hot chocolate

J'adore le chocolat chaud.
I love hot chocolate.

un jus d'orange
an orange juice

Vous avez du jus d'orange?
Have you got any orange juice?

un jus de pomme
an apple juice

Je préfère le jus de pomme.
I prefer apple juice.

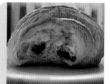

un pain au chocolat
a pain au chocolat (a type of chocolate pastry)

Manon mange un pain au chocolat.
Manon is eating a pain au chocolat.

un verre de lait
a glass of milk

Annie veut un verre de lait.
Annie wants a glass of milk.

une limonade
a lemonade

Une limonade pour moi, s'il vous plaît!
Lemonade for me, please!

3

Lesson 1: Going shopping

» How to say you are going shopping: *Je vais faire des courses.*

» How to ask if there's a bakery nearby: *Il y a une boulangerie près d'ici?*

» The names of different places to shop.

Lesson 2: The bus or the subway?

» How to say you don't know: *Je ne sais pas.*

» How to use the verb *prendre*.

» How to say something is faster: *C'est plus rapide*.

○ **Collins** | **Livemocha™**

UNIT 3 › LESSON 1
Going shopping

Culture note

The *boulangerie* is a bakery. Most *boulangeries* bake the bread on the premises and open at about 7 a.m. so you can buy fresh bread and croissants for breakfast. In France, fresh bread is usually served with every meal.

A *boulangerie* is usually open on Sunday morning but shut on a Monday. Most *boulangeries* also sell cakes but they are usually quite basic. For fancy cakes it is best to go to a *pâtisserie* where, on the other hand, you may not find bread. There are also many *boulangeries-pâtisseries* where you'll find the best of both.

Video Dialog

It's time to leave the café, so Pascal and the waiter give Mélinda directions to some local stores.

 Active French: Level 1 > Unit 3 > Lesson 1 > Video dialog

Mélinda:	*Merci pour le thé.*
Pascal:	*De rien. Vous allez où?*
Mélinda:	*Je vais faire des courses. Il y a une boulangerie près d'ici?*
Pascal:	*Oui, il y a une boulangerie à deux minutes d'ici.*
Mélinda:	*Et une librairie?*
Pascal:	*Je ne sais pas. Euh, monsieur, il y a une librairie près d'ici?*
Waiter:	*Comment?*
Pascal:	*Est-ce qu'il y a une librairie près d'ici?*
Waiter:	*Ben, non, la librairie la plus proche est boulevard St. Germain.*
Mélinda:	*C'est loin?*
Waiter:	*Ah oui, c'est loin d'ici. Il faut prendre le bus ou le métro.*

....

Mélinda:	Thanks for the tea.
Pascal:	Don't mention it. Where are you going?
Mélinda:	I'm going shopping. Is there a bakery near here?

55

Pascal:	Yes, there's a bakery just two minutes away.
Mélinda:	And a bookstore?
Pascal:	I don't know. Excuse me, is there a bookstore near here?
Waiter:	Pardon me?
Pascal:	Is there a bookstore near here?
Waiter:	No, the closest one is on boulevard St. Germain.
Mélinda:	Is it far?
Waiter:	Yes, it's far away. You'll have to take the bus or the subway.

Grammar

Active French: Level 1 > Unit 3 > Lesson 1 > Grammar

1 › **Where are you going?**

If you want to know where someone is going you use the word *où...* which means "where?"

> *Vous allez où?*
> Where are you going?

or if you are speaking to a friend:

> *Tu vas où?*
> Where are you going?

You can also say *où allez-vous?* or *où est-ce que vous allez?*

2 › **Going shopping**

> *Je vais faire des courses.*

Je vais means "I am going ..." and *faire* is the verb "to do" or "to make."

It is used in a lot of different expressions:

Je vais faire des courses.	I am going shopping.
Je vais faire une petite sieste.	I am going to take a little nap.
Je vais faire du tourisme.	I am going to tour around.

Watch out: *je vais faire **des** courses* means "I'm going shopping", but if you're going food shopping, you say *je vais faire **les** courses.*

3 › To do or to make

faire is the verb "to do" or "to make":

je fais	I am doing / making
tu fais	you are doing / making
il / elle fait	he / she is doing / making
nous faisons	we are doing / making
vous faites	you are doing / making
ils / elles font	they are doing / making

4 › There is or there are

Il y a means both "there is" and "there are":

Il y a une boulangerie en ville.
There is a bakery in town.

Il y a des magasins près d'ici.
There are some stores near here.

5 › Is there...?

> *Est-ce qu'il y a ...?*
> Is there ...?

Starting a sentence with *Est-ce que* ... is another way of asking a question:

Est-ce qu'il y a une pharmacie près d'ici?	Is there a pharmacy near here?
Est-ce qu'il y a un hôtel près d'ici?	Is there a hotel near here?
Est-ce qu'il y a des magasins près d'ici?	Are there any stores nearby?

Culture note

The boulevard St. Germain is a famous avenue on the south side of the river Seine, with many bookshops and cafés frequented by the students and professors from the nearby university.

6 › near and far

Près d'ici means "near here." *Loin d'ici* means "far from here."

C'est tout près.
It's very near.

C'est loin.
It's far (away).

7 › **Il faut – It is necessary**

Il faut is a very useful expression. As well as meaning "it is necessary," it can also be translated as:

you have to, I've got to, you ought to, we must, you need to …

It is usually followed by the infinitive:

Il faut aller …	You have to go …
Il faut prendre le bus.	You'll have to take the bus.
Il faut acheter son billet à l'avance.	You need to buy your ticket in advance.

8 › To ask someone to repeat something

To ask someone to repeat something you can say:

> *Comment?* or *Pardon?*
> I beg your pardon? Pardon?

Comment suggests that you did not catch what the person said.

> *Comment? Vous pouvez répéter?*
> Pardon? Can you repeat that?

Vocabulary

 Active French: Level 1 > Unit 3 > Lesson 1 > Vocabulary

la boulangerie
the bakery

On peut acheter du pain à la boulangerie.
You can buy bread at the bakery.

la pharmacie
the pharmacy

On achète des médicaments à la pharmacie.
You can buy medicine at the pharmacy.

la pâtisserie
the pastry shop

On peut acheter des gâteaux à la pâtisserie.
You can buy cakes at the pastry shop.

la boucherie
the butcher shop

On achète de la viande à la boucherie.
You buy meat at the butcher shop.

la librairie
the bookstore

On peut acheter des livres dans une librairie.
You can buy books from a bookstore.

le marché
the market

On peut acheter des fruits et des légumes au marché.
You can buy fruit and vegetables at the market.

le supermarché
the supermarket

On peut tout acheter au supermarché.
You can buy everything at the supermarket.

UNIT 3 › LESSON 2
The bus or the subway?

Culture note

La place de la Bastille marks the site of the former fortress prison. It was the storming of the Bastille on July 14, 1789 that marked the beginning of the French Revolution, and that day is still celebrated today as the French national day.

Today, the area of Bastille is very fashionable and has lots of cafés and restaurants. It also has an opera house, called *opéra Bastille*, which was inaugurated for the bicentenary of the French revolution in 1989 and has very modern architecture.

▶ *Video Dialog*

Pascal begins to give Mélinda some advice on public transportation but then he makes another decision.

 Active French: Level 1 > Unit 3 > Lesson 2 > Video dialog

Pascal:	*Alors, vous prenez le bus ou le métro?*
Mélinda:	*Je ne sais pas.*
Pascal:	*Le métro, c'est plus rapide.*
Mélinda:	*C'est direct?*
Pascal:	*Non, il faut changer à Bastille. Le bus, c'est plus direct.*
Mélinda:	*Je prends le bus alors.*
Pascal:	*C'est le 7. Et il faut descendre en haut du boulevard St. Germain.*
Mélinda:	*Où est l'arrêt de bus?*
Pascal:	*Juste en face. Attendez, je vous accompagne. Monsieur, l'addition, s'il vous plaît.*
Waiter:	*Ça fait 4 euros 70.*

....

Pascal:	Are you going to take the bus or the subway?
Mélinda:	I don't know.
Pascal:	The subway is quicker.
Mélinda:	Is it direct?
Pascal:	No, you have to change at Bastille. The bus is more direct.

Mélinda:	I'll take the bus, then.
Pascal:	It's the number 7 bus. You get off at the top of boulevard St. Germain.
Mélinda:	Where is the bus stop?
Pascal:	Just across the street. Wait, I'll go with you. The check, please.
Waiter:	That's 4 euros 70.

 Grammar

....

 Active French: Level 1 > Unit 3 > Lesson 2 > Grammar

1 › **Saying "I don't know"**

Pascal asks:

Vous prenez le bus ou le métro?

and Mélinda answers:

Je ne sais pas.

Je sais means "I know."

To make a negative in French and say you don't do something, you put a *ne ... pas* sandwich around the verb:

Je ne sais pas.	I don't know.
Je ne travaille pas à Paris.	I don't work in Paris.
Je ne prends pas le métro.	I'm not taking the subway.

2 › **Saying "I am taking the bus"**

Prendre is the verb "to take."

Pascal says:

> *Le bus, c'est plus direct.*

so Mélinda chooses to go by bus.

She says:

Je prends le bus alors.	I'll take the bus, then.
Vous prenez le bus?	Are you taking the bus?
Je prends le métro.	I am taking the subway.
Je prends le bus.	I am taking the bus.
Il déteste prendre l'avion.	He hates flying.

3 › **Prendre – to take**

je prends	I take
tu prends	you take
il / elle prend	he / she takes
nous prenons	we take
vous prenez	you take
ils / elles prennent	they take

4 › **It's faster**

plus rapide
faster

Plus means "more" and *rapide* means "fast."

So to make the comparative and say it is quicker you put *plus* in front of *rapide* and say *plus rapide*.

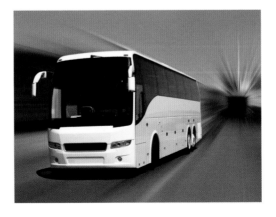

> ### *Le métro, c'est plus rapide.*
> The subway is faster.

> ### *Le bus, c'est plus direct.*
> The bus is more direct.

5 › **Giving instructions (1)**

> ### *il faut*
> you have to

One way to tell someone what to do is to use the expression: *il faut* – you have to.

Pascal says:

> ### *Il faut changer à Bastille.*
> You have to change at Bastille.

and:

> ### *Il faut descendre en haut du boulevard.*
> You have to get off at the top of the boulevard.

6 ›   **Giving instructions (2)**

Pascal then says:

> *Attendez, je vous accompagne.*
> Wait, I'll go with you.

Attendez!	Wait!
Descendez	Get off (the bus).
Allez tout droit.	Go straight ahead.

When you are giving instructions you can use the *vous* form of the verb without the *vous* and the verb usually ends in *-ez*.

You can also use the *tu* form if you know the person very well.

> *Attends! Prends le bus, c'est plus rapide.*

For some verbs, however, the *tu* ending *-s* is dropped. For example:

> *Écoute!*
> *Avance!*
> *Achète-moi le journal!*

7 › **Attendre – to wait**

j'attends	I wait
tu attends	you wait
il / elle attend	he / she waits
nous attendons	we wait
vous attendez	you wait
ils / elles attendent	they wait

Vocabulary

 Active French: Level 1 > Unit 3 > Lesson 2 > Vocabulary

le métro
the subway

Je prends le métro.
I am taking the subway.

la station de métro
the subway station

La station de métro est en face de l'hôtel.
The subway station is across from the hotel.

le train
the train

Le train c'est plus rapide.
The train is faster.

la gare SNCF
the train station

La gare SNCF est en face de la mairie.
The train station is across from city hall.

le bus
the bus

Je prends le bus.
I am taking the bus.

l'arrêt de bus
the bus stop

L'arrêt de bus est dans cette rue.
The bus stop is on this street.

le centre commercial
the shopping mall

Je fais des courses au centre commercial.
I shop at the mall.

l'addition
the check

L'addition, s'il vous plaît!
Can we have the check, please!

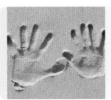

Numbers 0-10

0	1	2	3	4	5
zéro	un	deux	trois	quatre	cinq

6	7	8	9	10
six	sept	nuit	neuf	dix

4

Lesson 1: Eating out 1

» How to make suggestions using
on pourrait.
» How to say "too": *c'est trop cher / loin*.
» How to say what you like and prefer:
j'adore / je préfère.

Lesson 2: Eating out 2

» How to say the numbers from 11 to 50.
» How to say when places are open and
closed.
» How to use the 24-hour clock in French.

C **Collins** | Livemocha™

UNIT 4 › LESSON 1
Eating out 1

Culture note ⓘ

In Paris, some restaurants serving French food are quite expensive but others are reasonable. There are now lots of ethnic restaurants that are also very popular.

You will also now find a McDonald's in most French towns, but it has a slightly different menu with more salads to cater for French tastes.

French people call McDonald's *McDo*.

Video Dialog

Pascal and Mélinda discuss dinner options for the evening.

Active French: Level 1 > Unit 4 > Lesson 1 > Video dialog

Pascal:	*On pourrait dîner à l'hôtel ce soir.*
Mélinda:	*Oh non, c'est trop cher.*
Pascal:	*On pourrait aller à la pizzeria?*
Mélinda:	*C'est fermé ce soir.*
Pascal:	*On pourrait aller à la brasserie.*
Mélinda:	*Oh, c'est trop loin.*
Pascal:	*Qu'est-ce que tu préfères, alors?*
Mélinda:	*Je préfère un restaurant chinois.*
Pascal:	*Bonne idée, j'adore la cuisine chinoise.*
Mélinda:	*Moi aussi, j'adore ça.*

....

Pascal:	We could eat at the hotel tonight.
Mélinda:	No, it's too expensive.
Pascal:	We could go for a pizza.
Mélinda:	It's closed tonight.
Pascal:	We could go to the brasserie.
Mélinda:	Oh, it's too far.
Pascal:	What would you prefer, then?
Mélinda:	I would prefer a Chinese restaurant.
Pascal:	Good idea. I love Chinese food.
Mélinda:	Me too. I love it.

Grammar

. . . .

Active French: Level 1 > Unit 4 > Lesson 1 > Grammar

1 › How to make suggestions

> *On pourrait*
> We could

Pascal says:

> *On pourrait dîner à l'hôtel ce soir.*
> We could eat at the hotel this evening.

On pourrait means "one could" or "we could."

It is followed by the infinitive of the verb:

on pourrait aller	we could go
on pourrait dîner	we could eat

2 › **Too much**

Trop means "too."

Pascal suggests they eat at the hotel but Mélinda says:

> **Non, c'est trop cher.**
> No, it's too expensive.

He then suggests:

> **On pourrait aller à la brasserie.**
> We could go to the brasserie.

but she says:

> **Non, c'est trop loin.**
> No, it's too far.

3 › It's closed

Pascal suggests going to the pizzeria, but Mélinda says:

> *C'est fermé ce soir.*
> It's closed this evening.

ouvert means "open" and *fermé* means "closed".

4 › Position of the adjective

> *Il y a un restaurant chinois.*
> There is a Chinese restaurant.

In French, the adjective usually comes after the noun:

la cuisine chinoise	Chinese food
un restaurant chic	a chic restaurant
une famille française	a French family

There are some important exceptions to this rule.

Adjectives like *petit(e)* (small) and *grand(e)* (big) come in front of the noun:

une grande maison	a big house
un petit appartement	a small apartment
un beau quartier	a nice area
une jolie plage	a nice beach

5 › Regular *-er* verbs

Adorer – to love:

j'adore	I love
tu adores	you love
il / elle adore	he / she loves
nous adorons	we love
vous adorez	you love
ils / elles adorent	they love

Préférer – to prefer:

je préfère	I prefer
tu préfères	you prefer
il / elle préfère	he / she prefers
nous préférons	we prefer
vous préférez	you prefer
ils / elles préfèrent	they prefer

Note that the accents change for *nous* and *vous* and so does the pronunciation.

Mélinda says:

Je préfère un restaurant chinois.
I prefer a Chinese restaurant.

and Pascal agrees. He says:

> ### J'adore la cuisine chinoise.
> I love Chinese food.

These are called *-er* verbs because the infinitive ends in *-er*.

Most French verbs are *-er* verbs.

---

6 › **The endings of *-er* verbs**

All *-er* verbs (except *aller* – "to go") follow the same pattern.

After *je* the verb ends in *-e*.

je -e	*tu -es*	*il/elle -e*
nous -ons	*vous -ez*	*ils/elles -ent*

Although the ending varies, they all sound the same apart from the *nous* and *vous* forms.

85

7 ›   *Aller à...* to go to...

Note that the preposition *à* changes to *au* or *aux* according to what follows.

If the noun following is feminine, then use *à la...*; if it is masculine then use *au* (literally *à le*); and if it is plural, whether feminine or masculine, use *aux* (literally *à les*).

aller à la pizzeria	to go to the pizzeria
aller au restaurant	to go to the restaurant
aller aux toilettes	to go to the bathroom

Vocabulary

une pizzeria
pizzeria

On pourrait manger une pizza à la pizzeria.
We could have a pizza at the pizzeria.

un restaurant
restaurant

On pourrait dîner au restaurant.
We could have dinner at the restaurant.

une brasserie
brasserie (a type of restaurant, mainly in cities and big towns serving reasonably cheap food)

On pourrait aller à la brasserie.
We could go to the brasserie.

un burger
burger

Je voudrais un burger.
I would like a burger.

un sandwich
sandwich

un sandwich au jambon
a ham sandwich

un croque-monsieur
toasted ham sandwich with cheesy
white sauce on top

Pour moi, un croque-monsieur.
A toasted ham sandwich for me.

un steak frites
a steak with fries

Hugo veut un steak frites.
Hugo wants a steak with fries.

la salade
salad

Mélinda préfère de la salade.
Mélinda prefers a salad.

les légumes
vegetables

une soupe aux légumes
vegetable soup

la viande
meat

Je ne mange pas de viande.
I don't eat meat.

le poulet
chicken

Pascal prend du poulet.
Pascal has the chicken.

le poisson
fish

Delphine prend du poisson.
Delphine has the fish.

le fromage
cheese

J'adore le fromage.
I love cheese.

UNIT 4 › LESSON 2
Eating out 2

Culture note ⓘ

In France, people tend to use the 24-hour clock to tell the time.

If you're not used to it, it can be confusing.

13:30

Video Dialog

Pascal and Mélinda decide to find a Chinese restaurant for dinner. They run into the waiter from the café and ask his advice on where to go.

Active French: Level 1 > Unit 4 > Lesson 2 > Video dialog

Pascal:	*Ah! Bonjour, monsieur. Excusez-moi, est-ce qu'il y a un restaurant chinois près d'ici?*
Waiter:	*Oui, il y en a un à deux minutes d'ici. Ça s'appelle Le Bambou d'or.*
Pascal:	*Il ouvre à quelle heure?*
Waiter:	*Il ouvre à dix-huit heures … et il ferme à vingt-trois heures.*
Pascal:	*Est-ce qu'il faut réserver?*
Waiter:	*Oui, il faut réserver. Voici le numéro.*
Pascal:	*Merci.*
Waiter:	*De rien.*
Pascal:	*Allô, Le Bambou d'or? Oui, une table pour deux personnes … ce soir. À quelle heure? … vingt heures, bon, parfait. Mon nom? M. Berriot. Merci, au revoir. Voilà, c'est fait.*

. . . .

Pascal:	Ah! Hello. Excuse me, is there a Chinese restaurant near here?
Waiter:	Yes, there's one two minutes from here. It's called The Golden Bamboo.

Pascal:	What time does it open?
Waiter:	It opens at 6 p.m. ... and it shuts at 11 p.m.
Pascal:	Do I need reservations?
Waiter:	Yes, you need reservations. Here's the number.
Pascal:	Thanks.
Waiter:	Don't mention it.
Pascal:	Hello, The Golden Bamboo? Yes, a table for two this evening. What time? ... 8 p.m., good, perfect. My name? Mr. Berriot. Thank you. Goodbye. There, it's done.

Culture note

In France, when people ask your name in an official context, you always give your last name first rather than your first name. For example, if you have to fill out a form or if you take an exam you would always give your last name first.

Culture note

French people tend to have lunch between 12:30 p.m. and 2:30 p.m., and dinner from 8 p.m. onwards. Although some restaurants serve food all day, you would find most restaurants fairly quiet if you go out for dinner before 8 p.m.

Grammar

....

 Active French: Level 1 > Unit 4 > Lesson 2 > Grammar

1 › **Opening times**

ouvrir means "to open"
fermer means "to close"

> ### *Le restaurant ouvre à 18 h et ferme à 23 h.*
> The restaurant opens at 6 p.m. and closes at 11 p.m.

Culture note   *i*

After Pascal says *merci,* the waiter
answers *de rien* – "don't mention it."
Another way to express this would be *je
vous en prie.*
Merci, madame. – Thank you.
Je vous en prie. – Don't mention it.

2 › What time?

To ask what time something opens, closes, or starts, use the expression *à quelle heure*.

À quelle heure ouvre le restaurant?	What time does the restaurant open?
Ça ferme à quelle heure?	What time does it close?
À quelle heure commence le film?	What time does the movie start?

3 › The 24-hour clock 1

In France, people tend to use the 24-hour clock.

The waiter says the Chinese restaurant opens at *dix-huit heures*
18h00 = 1800 hours, 6 p.m.
and closes at *vingt-trois heures*.
23h00 = 2300 hours, 11 p.m.

Pascal books a table for *vingt heures*.
20h00 = 2000 hours, 8 p.m.

However, if you say *six heures* instead of *dix-huit heures*, people will still understand you.

4 › The 24-hour clock 2

1 p.m.	13h00	*treize heures*
2 p.m.	14h00	*quatorze heures*
3 p.m.	15h00	*quinze heures*
4 p.m.	16h00	*seize heures*
5 p.m.	17h00	*dix-sept heures*
6 p.m.	18h00	*dix-huit heures*
7 p.m.	19h00	*dix-neuf heures*
8 p.m.	20h00	*vingt heures*
9 p.m.	21h00	*vingt-et-une heures dix*
10 p.m.	22h00	*vingt-deux heures*
11 a.m.	23h00	*vingt-trois heures*

5 › The 24-hour clock 3

5:30 p.m.	17h30	*dix-sept heures trente*
6:15 p.m.	18h15	*dix-huit heures quinze*
7:20 p.m.	19h20	*dix-neuf heures vingt*
8:25 p.m.	20h25	*vingt heures vingt-cinq*
9:10 p.m.	21h10	*vingt-et-une heures dix*
10:40 p.m.	22h40	*vingt-deux heures quarante*
11:50 p.m.	23h50	*vingt-trois heures cinquante*
12 a.m.	24h00	*minuit*

Vocabulary

	onze eleven ***Il est onze heures.*** It's eleven o'clock.
	**douze** twelve ***douze œufs*** twelve eggs
	**treize** thirteen ***Le chiffre 13 porte malheur.*** The number 13 is bad luck.

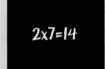

quatorze
fourteen

Deux fois sept égalent quatorze.
Two times seven is fourteen.

quinze
fifteen

une équipe de quinze joueurs
a team of fifteen players

seize
sixteen

Elle a seize ans.
She's sixteen years old.

dix-sept
seventeen

Il habite au numéro dix-sept.
He lives at number seventeen.

dix-huit
eighteen

Elle a dix-huit cousins.
She has eighteen cousins.

dix-neuf
nineteen

Il y a dix-neuf élèves dans la classe.
There are nineteen students in the class.

vingt
twenty

un bouquet de vingt roses
a bouquet of twenty roses

trente
thirty

un homme de trente ans
a thirty-year-old man

quarante
forty

Ils ne se sont pas vus pendant quarante ans.
They haven't seen each other in 40 years.

cinquante
fifty

un billet de cinquante euros
a fifty-euro bill

5

Lesson 1: My schedule

» The names of the days of the week.
» How to use the verb *travailler*.
» How to ask a question using:
Qu'est-ce que ...?

Lesson 2: Plan for the week

» About the gender of French nouns.
» How to translate the determiner "the":
le, la and *l'*.
» How to say "to the": *à + le, la* and *l'*.

○ **Collins** | Livemocha™

UNIT 5 › LESSON 1

My schedule

Video Dialog

Delphine asks Hugo about his plans for the coming week.

Active French: Level 1 > Unit 5 > Lesson 1 > Video dialog

Delphine:	*Qu'est-ce que tu fais la semaine prochaine?*
Hugo:	*Lundi, je travaille à l'agence.*
Delphine:	*Et mardi?*
Hugo:	*Mardi, j'ai rendez-vous avec un client à Lille.*
Delphine:	*Et mercredi?*
Hugo:	*Mercredi et jeudi, je travaille à l'agence.*
Delphine:	*Vendredi, tu travailles toute la journée?*
Hugo:	*Non, je finis à midi. L'après-midi, je fais des courses.*
Delphine:	*Et ce week-end? Qu'est-ce que tu fais ce week-end?*
Hugo:	*Samedi, je vais voir un match de foot.*
Delphine:	*Et dimanche?*
Hugo:	*Dimanche, je suis libre.*

Delphine:	What are you doing next week?
Hugo:	Monday I am working at the agency.
Delphine:	And Tuesday?
Hugo:	Tuesday I have a meeting with a client in Lille.
Delphine:	And Wednesday?
Hugo:	Wednesday and Thursday I am working at the agency.

Delphine:	Are you working all day on Friday?
Hugo:	No, I finish at noon. In the afternoon I'm going shopping.
Delphine:	And this weekend? What are you doing this weekend?
Hugo:	Saturday I am going to a soccer game.
Delphine:	And Sunday?
Hugo:	I'm free on Sunday.

Grammar

Active French: Level 1 > Unit 5 > Lesson 1 > Grammar

1 ›   **Work!**

travailler is the verb "to work." *travailler* is a regular *-er* verb (the infinitive ends with *-er*) so it follows the same pattern as *adorer*.

travailler	to work
je travaille	I work
tu travailles	you work
il / elle travaille	he / she works
nous travaillons	we work
vous travaillez	you work
ils / elles travaillent	they work

Hugo says:

> *Mercredi et jeudi je travaille à l'agence.*
> Wednesday and Thursday I am working at the agency.

Delphine asks:

> *Vendredi, tu travailles toute la journée?*
> Are you working all day Friday?

2 › **I work and I am working**

The present tense and the present continuous:
Je travaille means both "I work" and "I am working."

> ### Je travaille à New York.
> I work in New York.

And Hugo says:

> ### Lundi je travaille à l'agence.
> Monday I am working at the agency.

In French, to express something that you do regularly, you say:

> ### Le lundi, je vais à la bibliothèque.
> On Mondays I go to the library.

Adding *le* in front of the day of the week indicates that it is something you often do on that day.

> ### Le samedi, je fais les courses.
> On Saturdays, I do the food shopping.

> ### Le dimanche matin, je vais courir.
> Every Sunday morning, I go for a run.

3 › ## What?

Qu'est-ce que is a way to introduce a question.

As French does not have a present continuous form, *qu'est-ce que tu fais?* means both "what are you doing?" and "what do you do?"

Qu'est-ce que tu fais la semaine prochaine?	What are you doing next week?
Qu'est-ce que tu fais ce week-end?	What are you doing this weekend?
Qu'est-ce que tu fais le lundi?	What do you do on Mondays?

4 › ## Days of the week

Note that in French, the days of the week do not take an initial capital letter.

> *Qu'est-ce que tu fais lundi?*
> What are you doing on Monday?

5 ›   What day is it?

To ask what day it is, in French you say:

> *Quel jour sommes-nous?*
> (literally "What day are we?")

Or, in an informal context:

> *Quel jour on est?*

> *Nous sommes vendredi.*
> Today is Friday.

Culture note ⓘ

Franglais
There are lots of words that the French have borrowed from English. They are referred to as *franglais*.

A few examples: *le week-end, le brunch, le jogging*. The meaning of some words borrowed from English sometimes shifts from the original. For example, *planning* in French means "schedule" and *jogging* is used to describe a tracksuit as well as the activity of going for a jog.

The French authorities are trying to fight against too many English words invading the French language. For example, it is recommended to use the word *courriel* instead of *email*, although in reality French people will nearly always use *email*.

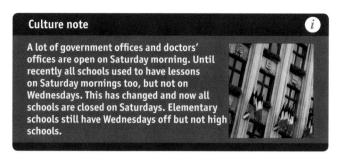

Culture note ⓘ

A lot of government offices and doctors' offices are open on Saturday morning. Until recently all schools used to have lessons on Saturday mornings too, but not on Wednesdays. This has changed and now all schools are closed on Saturdays. Elementary schools still have Wednesdays off but not high schools.

Vocabulary

 *Active French: Level 1 > Unit 5 > Lesson 1 > Vocabulary*

la semaine prochaine
next week

La semaine prochaine nous travaillons.
Next week we are working.

lundi
Monday

Lundi, je travaille au bureau.
Monday I am working in the office.

mardi
Tuesday

Mardi, j'ai rendez-vous avec un client.
Tuesday I have a meeting with a client.

mercredi
Wednesday

Mercredi, je vais à Washington.
Wednesday I'm going to Washington.

jeudi
Thursday

Jeudi, je retourne à New York.
Thursday I'm going back to New York.

vendredi
Friday

Vendredi soir, on se retrouve au bar.
Friday evening we're meeting at the bar.

samedi
Saturday

Samedi, Isabelle travaille au restaurant.
Saturday Isabelle is working in the restaurant.

dimanche
Sunday

Le dimanche on fait la grasse matinée.
On Sundays we sleep in.

un rendez-vous
appointment

J'ai rendez-vous chez le dentiste.
I have an appointment at the dentist.

la journée
day

Je travaille toute la journée.
I work all day.

le matin
morning

Dimanche matin, je fais la grasse matinée.
On Sunday morning, I sleep in.

le midi
lunchtime

Le midi, je déjeune au café.
At lunchtime I have lunch in the café.

midi
noon

Je finis mon travail à midi.
I finish working at noon.

l'après-midi
afternoon

Qu'est-ce que tu fais cet après-midi?
What are you doing this afternoon?

le soir
evening

Ce soir, nous allons au restaurant.
This evening, we're going out to a restaurant.

UNIT 5 › LESSON 2

Plan for the week

Culture note ⓘ

In France, most stores are closed on Sundays. Outside big cities, stores usually close at lunchtime for a couple of hours, but they stay open until at least 7 p.m. (often 8 p.m. if they sell food).

Video Dialog

Now it's Delphine's turn to tell Hugo what she has planned for the coming week.

 Active French: Level 1 > Unit 5 > Lesson 2 > Video dialog

Hugo:	*Et toi, qu'est-ce que tu fais la semaine prochaine?*
Delphine:	*Lundi et mardi, je travaille à la boutique.*
Hugo:	*Mercredi?*
Delphine:	*Mercredi et jeudi, j'ai des rendez-vous avec des clients en ville.*
Hugo:	*Vendredi, je suis libre l'après-midi. Et toi?*
Delphine:	*Vendredi, j'ai des clients toute la journée.*
Hugo:	*Et ce week-end?*
Delphine:	*Samedi matin, je travaille à la boutique, mais l'après-midi je suis libre.*
Hugo:	*Tu veux venir au match de foot avec moi, samedi après-midi?*
Delphine:	*Sûrement pas!*

....

Hugo:	And you, what are you doing next week?
Delphine:	Monday and Tuesday I am working in the shop.
Hugo:	Wednesday?
Delphine:	Wednesday and Thursday I have meetings with clients in town.
Hugo:	Friday I am free in the afternoon. And you?

Delphine:	Friday I have clients all day.
Hugo:	And this weekend?
Delphine:	Saturday morning I am working in the shop, but in the afternoon I am free.
Hugo:	Do you want to come to the soccer game with me on Saturday afternoon?
Delphine:	No way!

Grammar

Active French: Level 1 > Unit 5 > Lesson 2 > Grammar

1 › **Masculine or feminine?**

In French all nouns are either masculine or feminine.

Unfortunately you can't tell whether a word is going to be masculine or feminine; you just have to learn them as you go along.

The word for "the" is *le* with masculine nouns and *la* with feminine nouns:

le café	the café
la boulangerie	the baker's

2 › Masculine nouns

You have already seen some masculine words in previous lessons:

le bureau	the office
le restaurant	the restaurant
le bar	the bar
le café	the café
le bus	the bus
le métro	the subway
le jour	the day
le week-end	the weekend
le match de foot	the soccer game
le stade	the stadium

3 › Feminine nouns

Here are some feminine words you have already seen in previous lessons:

la journée	the whole day
la pizzeria	the pizzeria
la librairie	the bookstore
la ville	the town
la station de métro	the subway station

4 › Using *l'*

If a word begins with a vowel or silent "h," you use *l'* instead of *le* or *la*:

l'agence	the agency
l'idée	the idea
l'ascenseur	the elevator
l'hôtel	the hotel

5 › *à* means "to" or "at"

When you use *à* in front of a masculine noun *à + le* becomes *au*.

Hugo invites Delphine to a soccer game:

> *Tu veux venir au match de foot?*
> Do you want to come to the soccer game?

à doesn't change with feminine words and words that begin with a vowel.

Delphine says:

> *Je travaille à la boutique.*
> I work in the shop.

When Mélinda is going back to the hotel she says:

> *Je rentre à l'hôtel.*
> I'm going back to the hotel.

Vocabulary

 Active French: Level 1 > Unit 5 > Lesson 2 > Vocabulary

l'agence
the agency

Hugo travaille dans une agence immobilière.
Hugo works at a real estate office.

la banque
the bank

Patrice travaille à la banque.
Patrice works at the bank.

le bureau
the office

Mme Duval travaille dans un bureau.
Mrs. Duval works in an office.

la gare
the train station

Où est la gare, s'il vous plaît?
Where is the train station, please?

l'hôtel
the hotel

L'hôtel est dans cette rue.
The hotel is on this street.

la mairie
the city hall

La mairie est sur la place du marché.
The city hall is on the market square.

la poste
the post office

La poste est en face de la mairie.
The post office is across from city hall.

la station de métro
the subway station

La station de métro est à deux minutes d'ici.
The subway station is two minutes from here.

le marché
the market

Il y a un marché sur cette place tous les vendredis.
There's a market in this square every Friday.

6

Lesson 1: Getting takeout 1

- » How to make suggestions using *on pourrait*.
- » How to talk about food: *une pizza, une salade verte ...*
- » How to say "at my place": *chez moi.*

Lesson 2: Getting takeout 2

- » How to say something was delicious: *C'était délicieux.*
- » How to ask if people would like some more: *encore ...?*
- » How to say "some" or "any."

Collins | **Livemocha™**

UNIT 6 › LESSON 1
Getting takeout 1

Culture note

The concept of takeout meals is not hugely developed in France. In big cities you can find pizza and Chinese meals to take out, but in smaller places it may be difficult.

Video Dialog

Hugo and Delphine make some plans for the evening.

 Active French: Level 1 > Unit 6 > Lesson 1 > Video dialog

Hugo:	*On pourrait dîner ensemble?*
Delphine:	*C'est mercredi. Le resto est fermé ce soir.*
Hugo:	*Tu pourrais venir chez moi. J'achèterai des pizzas à emporter.*
Delphine:	*D'accord ... et moi, je peux apporter une salade verte et du vin.*
Hugo:	*Qu'est-ce que tu veux comme pizza?*
Delphine:	*Euh ... une pizza reine.*
Hugo:	*Je pourrais aussi louer un DVD.*
Delphine:	*OK. À ce soir.*

....

Hugo:	Shall we eat together this evening?
Delphine:	It's Wednesday. The restaurant is closed this evening.
Hugo:	You could come to my place. I'll get takeout pizza.
Delphine:	Okay ... and I'll bring a green salad and some wine.
Hugo:	What sort of pizza do you want?
Delphine:	Er ... I'll have ham and mushroom.
Hugo:	And I could rent a DVD.
Delphine:	Okay. See you tonight.

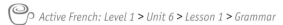

Grammar

Active French: Level 1 > Unit 6 > Lesson 1 > Grammar

1 › **Making suggestions**

On pourrait – "we could" – is followed by the infinitive.

Hugo says:

On pourrait dîner ensemble.	We could have dinner together.
Tu pourrais venir chez moi.	You could come to my place.
On pourrait aller au cinéma.	We could go to the movies.
On pourrait louer un DVD.	We could rent a DVD.

2 › **Eating and dining**

The evening meal is *le dîner* in France. The word *dîner* can mean either "dinner" or "to have dinner."

> *Tu veux dîner avec moi ce soir?*
> Would you like to have dinner with me tonight?

> *Je dîne à vingt heures.*
> I eat at 8 p.m.

3 › *Chez moi*

Chez moi means "at my house" or "at my place" if you live in an apartment.

chez le boulanger	at the baker's
chez mon ami	at my friend's
chez toi / chez vous	at your place
On se retrouve chez toi?	Shall we meet at your place?
Tu es chez toi?	Are you at home?

4 › Accented letters

You may have noticed different accents on some of the letters. Most of them do not affect the sound of the letter, but these two do: *é* and *è*.

é: e has an acute accent or *accent aigu* and sounds like "ay."
è: e has a grave accent or *accent grave* and sounds like "eh."

é	*ay*	*café*
è	*eh*	*achète*

je préfère has both of them.

5 › to carry, to bring, to take

porter, apporter and *emporter*
porter means "to wear" or "to carry."

> ### *Elle porte un pull rouge.*
> She is wearing a red sweater.

> ### *Je peux porter ta valise.*
> I can carry your suitcase.

apporter means "to bring."

Delphine says:

> ### *Je peux apporter une salade.*
> I can bring a salad.

emporter means "to take away" or "to carry away."

Hugo says he will buy:

> *une pizza à emporter*
> a takeaway pizza

> *N'oublie pas d'emporter un manteau.*
> Don't forget to take a coat with you.

porter is a regular *-er* verb:

je porte	I wear / carry
tu portes	you wear / carry
il / elle porte	he / she wears / carries
nous portons	we wear / carry
vous portez	you wear / carry
ils / elles portent	they wear / carry

and any verbs made from *porter* (e.g. *apporter, emporter, comporter*) behave in the same way.

6 › How to express the future

Hugo says:

> *J'achèterai des pizzas.*
> I will buy some pizzas.

The endings for future forms of French verbs are the same for most verbs (except for *aller, être, avoir*):

j'achèterai	I will buy
tu achèteras	you will buy
il / elle achètera	he / she will buy
nous achèterons	we will buy
vous achèterez	you will buy
ils / elles achèteront	they will buy

7 › *aller*

j'irai	I will go
tu iras	you will go
il / elle ira	he / she will go
nous irons	we will go
vous irez	you will go
ils / elles iront	they will go

8 › *être*

je serai	I will be
tu seras	you will be
il / elle sera	he / she will be
nous serons	we will be
vous serez	you will be
ils / elles seront	they will be

9 › *avoir*

j'aurai	I will have
tu auras	you will have
il / elle aura	he / she will have
nous aurons	we will have
vous aurez	you will have
ils / elles auront	they will have

Culture note

A French meal usually consists of a starter, such as salad or cold meats with fresh bread, then a main course of meat or fish with vegetables. After the main course and before the dessert comes cheese. Finally there will be fruit or a dessert such as mousse or yogurt.

Vocabulary

le pain
bread

Je voudrais du pain.
I would like some bread.

la soupe
soup

Pascal mange de la soupe.
Pascal is eating some soup.

le fromage
cheese

Hugo voudrait du fromage.
Hugo wants some cheese.

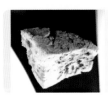

une pizza
pizza

Il achète une pizza à emporter.
He is buying a takeout pizza.

la salade (verte)
green salad, lettuce

Delphine prépare une salade verte.
Delphine is making a green salad.

le vin
wine

Hugo offre un verre de vin rouge à Delphine.
Hugo offers Delphine a glass of red wine.

un dessert
a dessert

Delphine ne veut pas de dessert.
Delphine doesn't want a dessert.

un DVD
a DVD

Hugo loue un DVD.
Hugo rents a DVD.

un CD
a CD

Ils écoutent un CD.
They're listening to a CD.

UNIT 6 › LESSON 2
Getting takeout 2

Culture note ℹ

Du camembert
It used to be said that there was a different French cheese for
every day of the year. As well as the many local cheeses there are
56 cheeses which are officially recognized and legally protected.
Camembert is one of these. It is a soft cheese that is made in
Normandy, in the northwest of France, a region famous for its
farming, especially dairy cattle and good milk. *Brie* is another
famous soft cheese from the Paris area. *Comté* and *Beaufort* are
two notable hard cheeses from eastern France, and *Roquefort* is
a famous blue cheese from the south. French people always eat
cheese with bread as opposed to crackers. On restaurant menus,
there is often a choice of *fromage ou dessert* – cheese or dessert.
Restaurants sometimes offer *fromage blanc* (a fresh cheese
sometimes called *fromage frais* in English) served in a small bowl
and eaten either with salt and pepper or sugar.

Video Dialog

Hugo and Delphine are finishing their pizza and settling down to watch a DVD.

 Active French: Level 1 > Unit 6 > Lesson 2 > Video dialog

Delphine:	*C'était délicieux.*
Hugo:	*Encore un peu de salade?*
Delphine:	*Non, merci.*
Hugo:	*Tu veux du fromage? J'ai un bon Camembert.*
Delphine:	*Merci, j'ai assez mangé.*
Hugo:	*Encore un verre de vin?*
Delphine:	*Pourquoi pas?*
Hugo:	*Santé.*
Delphine:	*Santé.*
Hugo:	*Un petit café?*
Delphine:	*Je veux bien.*
Hugo:	*Du sucre?*
Delphine:	*Tu as des sucrettes?*
Hugo:	*Voilà. Maintenant on peut regarder le DVD!*

Delphine:	That was delicious!
Hugo:	Would you like some more salad?
Delphine:	No, thanks.

Hugo:	Would you like some cheese? I've got a great Camembert.
Delphine:	No, thanks. I've had enough.
Hugo:	Some more wine?
Delphine:	Why not?
Hugo:	Cheers.
Delphine:	Cheers.
Hugo:	Coffee?
Delphine:	Yes please.
Hugo:	Sugar?
Delphine:	Do you have any sweeteners?
Hugo:	Here you are. Now we can watch the DVD!

Grammar

 Active French: Level 1 > Unit 6 > Lesson 2 > Grammar

1 ›   Saying what something was like:

Delphine says:

> *C'était délicieux.*
> It was delicious.

C'était means "it was."

> ### *C'était délicieux.*
> It was delicious.

> ### *C'était parfait.*
> It was perfect.

More?

Encore can mean "still" or "again," but in this context, it means "more."

Hugo asks:

> ### *Encore un peu de salade?*
> Would you like some more salad?

And:

> ### *Encore un verre de vin?*
> Another glass of wine?

He could also say:

> ### *Est-ce que tu veux encore un peu de vin?*
> Would you like some more wine?

3 › How to say "some"

The word for "some" is *de*.

de + le = du

> ### *du fromage*
> some cheese

In French, you can't just say "Do you want cheese?"; you have to add the word for "some":

> ### *Tu veux du fromage?*
> Do you want (some) cheese?

In the plural *de + les = des*

> ### *des sucrettes*
> sweeteners

Tu as des sucrettes?
Have you got any sweeteners?

de + *la* and *de* + *l'* don't change:

Encore de la salade?
Do you want more salad?

Il y a de l'ail dans la sauce.
There's garlic in the sauce.

4 › **Enough**

The word for "enough" is *assez*.

J'ai assez mangé.	I have eaten enough.
J'ai eu assez de salade.	I've had enough salad.
Je n'ai pas assez dormi.	I haven't slept long enough, I haven't had enough sleep.

141

abc *Vocabulary*

. . . .

 *Active French: Level 1 > Unit 6 > Lesson 2 > Vocabulary*

un verre de vin
a glass of wine

Je voudrais un verre de vin.
I would like a glass of wine.

vin rouge
red wine

un verre de vin rouge
a glass of red wine

vin blanc
white wine

un verre de vin blanc
a glass of white wine

un verre d'eau
a glass of water

Je peux avoir un verre d'eau?
Can I have a glass of water?

une bouteille
a bottle

Vous avez une bouteille de vin rouge?
Do you have a bottle of red wine?

le champagne
champagne

Je vais apporter une bouteille de champagne.
I am bringing a bottle of champagne.

l'eau gazeuse
sparkling mineral water, seltzer

Delphine veut une bouteille d'eau gazeuse.
Delphine wants a bottle of seltzer.

l'eau plate
still water (not carbonated)

Mélinda préfère une bouteille d'eau plate.
Mélinda prefers a bottle of still water.